table-runner roundup

13 Quilted Projects to Spice Up Your Table

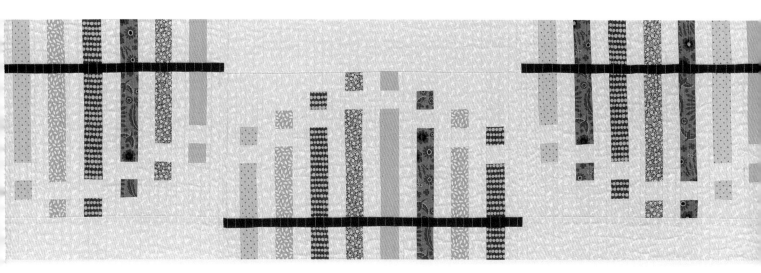

COMPILED BY AMELIA JOHANSON

Martingale®
Create with Confidence

Table-Runner Roundup:
13 Quilted Projects to Spice Up Your Table
© 2018 by Martingale & Company®

Martingale®
19021 120th Ave. NE, Ste. 102
Bothell, WA 98011-9511 USA
ShopMartingale.com

Printed in China
23 22 21 20 19 18   8 7 6 5 4 3 2 1

Library of Congress Cataloging-in-Publication Data
is available upon request.

ISBN: 978-1-60468-937-2

MISSION STATEMENT

We empower makers who use fabric and yarn
to make life more enjoyable.

CREDITS

PUBLISHER AND
CHIEF VISIONARY OFFICER
Jennifer Erbe Keltner

CONTENT DIRECTOR
Karen Costello Soltys

DESIGN MANAGER
Adrienne Smitke

MANAGING EDITOR
Tina Cook

PRODUCTION MANAGER
Regina Girard

ACQUISITIONS EDITOR
Amelia Johanson

INTERIOR DESIGNER
Angie Hoogensen

TECHNICAL WRITER
Elizabeth Beese

COVER DESIGNER
Kathy Kotomaimoce

TECHNICAL EDITOR
Debra Finan

STUDIO PHOTOGRAPHER
Brent Kane

COPY EDITOR
Durby Peterson

LOCATION PHOTOGRAPHER
Adam Albright

ILLUSTRATORS
Sandy Loi
Missy Shepler

contents

Introduction 5

PROJECTS
Scrappy Stars » *Jude Spero* 7
Detachable Hexagons » *Jane Davidson* 9
Pineapple Parade » *Deane Beesley* 15
All Lined Up » *Tony Jacobson* 19
Hightail » *Kim Lapacek* 23
Farm Fresh » *Sue Pfau* 29
Improv Under Control » *Miranda Rosa* 33
Making Waves » *Julie Taylor* 37
Star-in-a-Star » *Julie Taylor* 43
Moving Along » *Tony Jacobson* 47
Equinox » *Michelle Bartholomew* 51
Wonky Triangles » *Miranda Rosa* 55
Olive Tree » *Annette Ornelas* 57

About the Contributors 64

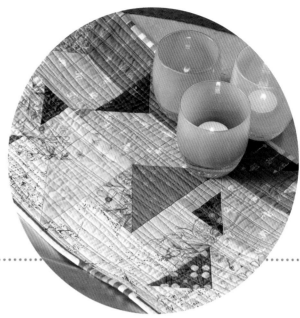

introduction

Quilters know that warming a home is only a couple hours and few favorite fabrics away, because a swath of patchwork draped atop any surface doesn't just brighten a room—it adds color to our lives.

Like you, here at Martingale we're drawn to table toppers. Some intrigue us with unique fabric combinations, and others by unexpected shapes, but each and every one offers the benefit of being an achievable, start-to-finish project that fits into our bustling schedules.

We've rounded up 13 fresh patterns from familiar friends and up-and-coming designers to render an unexpected collection that juxtaposes homespun tradition with bold, minimalist options. There are no limits. Who says you can't top a farmhouse table with the Equinox runner (page 51)—a Southwestern twist of pastel half-square triangles? Or toss the traditional Scrappy Stars runner (page 7) over a modern kitchen island? In fact, we know of no rule that demands table toppers stay in the kitchen or even on top of a table. Why not embellish a vanity, dress up a dresser, or display a runner on an otherwise sparse patch of wall space?

Along with an impactful mix of typically sized runners are a few unexpected treasures. One of our favorites is Jane Davidson's quad of Detachable Hexagons (page 9). Button them together to make a runner or use them unbuttoned as place mats—so clever.

You're also likely to find some fun new techniques to add to your repertoire. Turn back the fabric on a bias fold to create the fabulous curved effects on the Olive Tree runner (page 57). Or insert triangles of different shapes and sizes inside square blocks to make the Wonky Triangles runner (page 55)—simply layer, slash, swap, and sew the pieces back together. It's ingenious!

Whether you prefer to use the color palettes shown, or reinterpret the patterns to reflect the colors and fabrics that suit your personal surroundings, dare we say, the possibilities truly are endless! So don't be surprised if, when you flip through these pages, you're suddenly hit with desire to perk up all your unadorned surfaces. We get it, because so are we.

scrappy stars

Splashes of red appear in the binding, borders, and blocks in this generously sized runner, giving it a cohesive look. When creating scrappy blocks, grab a variety of your favorite scraps and look for a unifying color to use throughout for a successful design. » **BY JUDE SPERO**

>> **Finished table runner:** 25½" × 76½"
Finished block: 12" × 12"

materials

Yardage is based on 42"-wide fabric.

- 48 squares, 3½" × 3½", of assorted prints for stars
- ⅝ yard of white solid for block backgrounds
- 1 yard of navy print for setting triangles
- ¾ yard of red print for inner border and binding
- ⅝ yard of navy-and-yellow floral for outer border
- 2½ yards of fabric for backing
- 32" × 83" piece of batting

cutting

All measurements include ¼"-wide seam allowances.

From the white solid, cut:
5 strips, 3½" × 42"; crosscut into:
    16 rectangles, 3½" × 6½"
    16 squares, 3½" × 3½"

From the navy print, cut:
2 squares, 18¼" × 18¼"; cut the squares into quarters
    diagonally to yield 8 side setting triangles
    (2 are extra)
2 squares, 9½" × 9½"; cut the squares in half diagonally
    to yield 4 corner setting triangles

From the red print, cut:
6 strips, 2½" × 42"
5 strips, 1½" × 42"

From the navy-and-yellow floral, cut:
5 strips, 3½" × 42"

making the blocks

Press all seam allowances as shown by the arrows in the illustrations.

1 Draw a diagonal line from corner to corner on the wrong side of 32 assorted print 3½" squares. Place a marked square on one end of a white 3½" × 6½" rectangle, right sides together. Stitch on the line; trim away the excess fabric, leaving a ¼" seam allowance; press.

2 In the same manner, place a second marked square on the opposite end of the unit made in step 1. Stitch, trim, and press to complete a flying-geese unit that measures 3½" × 6½", including seam allowances. Make 16 flying-geese units.

Make 16 units,
3½" × 6½".

3 Lay out four assorted print 3½" squares as shown. Sew them together into two pairs. Join the pairs to make a four-patch unit. Make four four-patch units that measure 6½" square, including seam allowances.

Make 4 units,
6½" × 6½".

4 Arrange a four-patch unit, four flying-geese units, and four white 3½" squares in rows as shown. Sew the pieces together in each row. Join the rows to make a Star block. Make four blocks that measure 12½" square, including seam allowances.

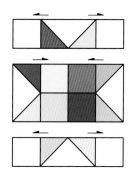 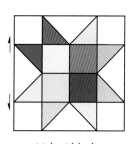

Make 4 blocks,
12½" × 12½".

assembling the table-runner top

1 Lay out the blocks and navy side and corner setting triangles as shown in the runner assembly diagram. Join the pieces into diagonal rows. Join the rows, and add the remaining corner triangles to make a table-runner center that measures 17½" × 68½", including seam allowances.

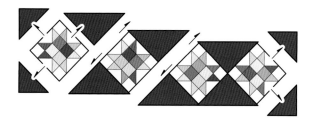

Runner assembly

2 Join the red 1½"-wide strips to make two 68½"-long and two 19½"-long inner borders. Sew the long borders to the long sides of the table-runner center. Add the short borders to the short sides.

3 Piece the floral 3½"-wide strips to make two 70½"-long and two 25½"-long outer borders. Sew the long outer borders to the table-runner center first, then add the short borders to the short sides to complete the table-runner top, which should measure 25½" × 76½".

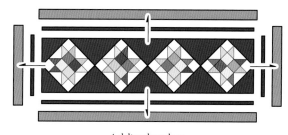

Adding borders

finishing the table runner

For help with the following steps, find free, illustrated instructions at ShopMartingale.com/HowtoQuilt.

1 Prepare a backing that's approximately 32" × 83". Layer the backing, batting, and table-runner top; baste together.

2 Hand or machine quilt; the runner shown is machine quilted with a grid design in the blocks, feathers in the navy triangles, and parallel lines plus a flower motif in the outer border.

3 Use the red 2½"-wide strips to make the binding, and then attach it to the runner.

detachable hexagons

Please pass the versatility! Cleverly planned to maximize both form and function, this unusual design works beautifully as either a runner or individual place mats. Easily shorten or lengthen it to suit your table— and feast on the possibilities. » **BY JANE DAVIDSON**

» **Finished table runner:** 11¼" × 54"
Finished place mat: 11¼" × 13¼"

materials

Yardage is based on 42"-wide fabric.

- 2 strips, 2¾" × 42", of assorted medium blue prints for blocks

- 1 strip, 1½" × 42", of green print for blocks

- 3 strips, 3½" × 42", of assorted navy prints for blocks

- 5 strips, 2" × 42", of assorted light blue prints for blocks

- 2 strips, 2½" × 42", of assorted coral prints for blocks*

- 1 yard of coral print for backing (This will be turned to the front to form the binding, so choose the color accordingly.)

- 30" × 30" square of batting

- 1½ yards of navy ⅛"-wide ribbon

- Chenille or tapestry needle with an eye wide enough for the ribbon

- 8 buttons, ⅝" diameter

- 60° ruler or clear template plastic

*If strips aren't 42" wide after removing selvages, you'll need 3 strips. Or cut 2 rectangles from backing-fabric scraps.

cutting

All measurements include ¼"-wide seam allowances.

From the assorted medium blue strips, cut:
48 rectangles, 1½" × 2¾"

From the green print, cut:
24 squares, 1½" × 1½"

From the assorted navy strips, cut:
48 rectangles, 2" × 3½"

From the assorted light blue strips, cut:
24 rectangles, 2" × 4½"
24 squares, 2" × 2"

From the assorted coral strips, cut:
24 rectangles, 2½" × 3½"

From the backing fabric, cut:
4 squares, 17" × 17"

From the batting, cut:
4 squares, 15" × 15"

making the hexagons

Press all seam allowances open.

1. Sew two medium blue 1½" × 2¾" rectangles to a green 1½" square as shown. Repeat to make a total of 24 units that measure 1½" × 6".

Make 24 units,
1½" × 6".

2. Sew two navy 2" × 3½" rectangles to a light blue 2" square as shown. Repeat to make a total of 24 units that measure 2" × 8".

Make 24 units,
2" × 8".

3 Lay out a coral 2½" × 3½" rectangle, a light blue 2" × 4½" rectangle, a unit from step 1, and a unit from step 2 as shown. Finger-press each piece in half. Matching the fold lines, join the pieces. Repeat to make a total of 24 units.

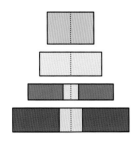 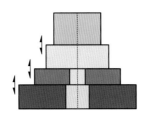

Make 24 units.

4 Position a 60° ruler with the 6" reference line at the base of the block. Make sure the ruler is centered. (If not using a ruler, make a template from the triangle pattern on page 13 and use that as a guide to cut triangles.) Cut 24 triangles.

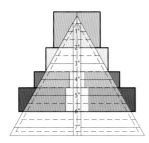 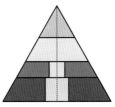

Make 24 triangles.

center of attention

If making your own 60° triangle template, be sure to mark the vertical centerline on it so you can easily and accurately cut the triangles.

5 Sew together two pieced triangles from tip to tip, making sure to match seam intersections. Add a third triangle to make a half hexagon. Make two half hexagons, and then join them to make a pieced hexagon. Repeat to make four pieced hexagons.

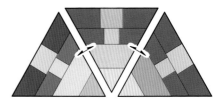

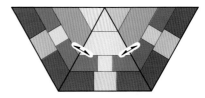

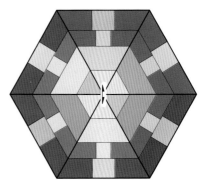

Make 4 units.

assembling and finishing the table runner

1 Lay a pieced hexagon on a 15" square of batting. Trim the batting to the same size as the hexagon. Center the hexagon and batting on a 17" square of backing fabric. Baste the layers together. Repeat with remaining pieced hexagons.

2 Hand or machine quilt; each hexagon shown is machine quilted with a loop and swirl design.

3 Trim each backing square ¾" beyond the edges of the hexagon.

4 Fold one backing edge to meet the edge of the hexagon; then fold over again, covering the raw edge of the hexagon. Pin or clip in place. Continue to fold each edge of the backing to the right side, making a miter at each corner. Do not sew the binding in place yet.

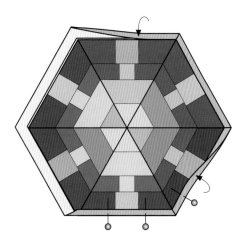

⌄ perfect binding

To achieve neat binding, steam press the folds of the binding. Use a heat-resistant hemming ruler to help ensure an accurate ¼" fold. Also, apply fabric glue or use clips to secure the folded binding as you stitch, which will make the job easier.

• • • • • •

5 Cut the ribbon into eight 6½" lengths. Thread a chenille needle with one length of ribbon and knot the remaining end. Insert the needle into a mitered corner of the hexagon and pull gently until the knot stops the ribbon from going through the fabric. Insert the needle back into the mitered corner, making a loop. Pull the loop until it will just fit over a ⅝"-diameter button. Pin the tails of the ribbon in place and trim the excess. Repeat to pin a ribbon loop to the opposite corner of the hexagon. Repeat with the remaining three quilted hexagons.

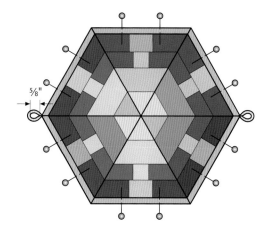

6 Using a small hand stitch or decorative machine stitch, sew the folded edge of the binding in place, securing the ribbon ends. Sew a button to each mitered corner that has a loop to complete four place mats.

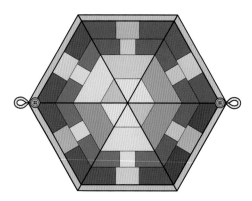

7 To form the table runner, link the place mats by placing each loop over the button of the adjacent place mat.

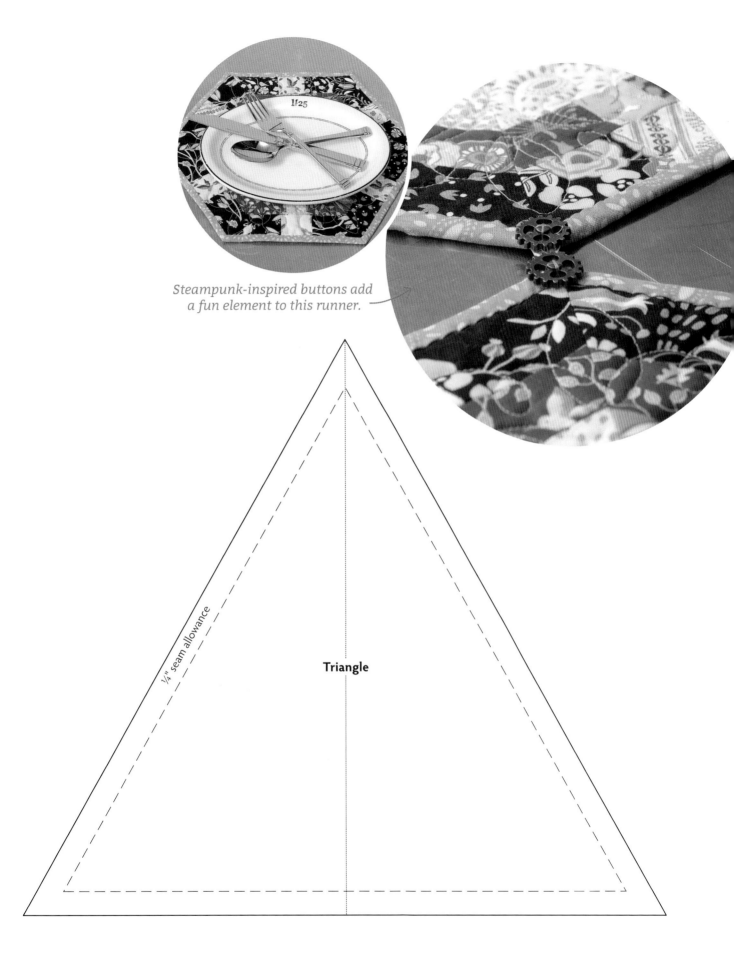

Steampunk-inspired buttons add a fun element to this runner.

Triangle

¼" seam allowance

pineapple parade

Pineapples are perfect for the patio table on hot summer days. Echo quilted to give dimension, these pineapples stand out on a background of cream prints. Touches of red in the background fabrics flip-flop from block to block, moving your eye along the runner. **» BY DEANE BEESLEY**

Finished table runner: 12½" × 40½"
Finished block: 8½" × 12½"

materials

Yardage is based on 42"-wide fabric.

- ¼ yard *each* of 4 assorted cream prints for background
- 1 rectangle, 5½" × 7½", *each* of 3 yellow and 2 red prints for pineapple appliqués
- ⅛ yard *each* of 2 green prints for leaf appliqués
- ⅓ yard of red print for binding
- 1 yard of fabric for backing
- 17" × 45" piece of batting
- ⅔ yard of 17"-wide lightweight paper-backed fusible web

cutting

All measurements include ¼"-wide seam allowances.

From *each* cream print, cut:
2 strips, 2½" × 42" (8 total); crosscut each strip into 4 rectangles, 2½" × 8½" (32 total; 2 are extra)

From the red print for binding, cut:
3 strips, 2½" × 42"

making the blocks

Press all seam allowances as shown by the arrows in the illustrations. For illustrated information on fusible appliqué, go to ShopMartingale.com/HowtoQuilt.

1 Sew together six assorted cream 2½" × 8½" rectangles to make a block background that measures 8½" × 12½", including seam allowances. Make a total of five units for block backgrounds.

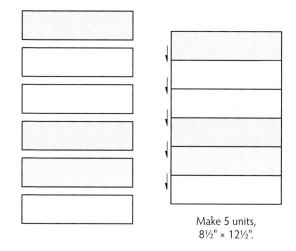

Make 5 units,
8½" × 12½".

2 Using the patterns on page 17, prepare the shapes for fusible appliqué.

3 Position a block background with the seam allowances pressed toward the bottom. Arrange the prepared shapes on the background as shown. Follow the manufacturer's instructions to fuse the shapes in place. Stitch around each appliqué using a zigzag stitch, blanket stitch, or stitch of your choice to permanently attach the shapes to the background. Repeat to appliqué five blocks.

Make 5 blocks,
8½" × 12½".

cut out the centers

To make the blocks less stiff and bulky, cut away the center of the pineapple fusible web, leaving only about ½" around the perimeter. It's enough to securely hold the shape in place.

· · · · · ·

assembling the table-runner top

Lay out the blocks as shown. Join the blocks to make the table-runner top, which should measure 12½" × 40½".

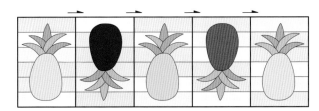

Runner assembly

finishing the table runner

For help with the following steps, find free, illustrated instructions at ShopMartingale.com/HowtoQuilt.

1 Prepare the backing so it's about 4" larger in both directions than the table-runner top. Layer the backing, batting, and table-runner top; baste the layers together.

2 Hand or machine quilt; the runner shown is machine quilted with crosshatching on the pineapples and echo quilting in the background around the pineapples.

3 Use the red 2½"-wide strips to make the binding, and then attach it to the runner.

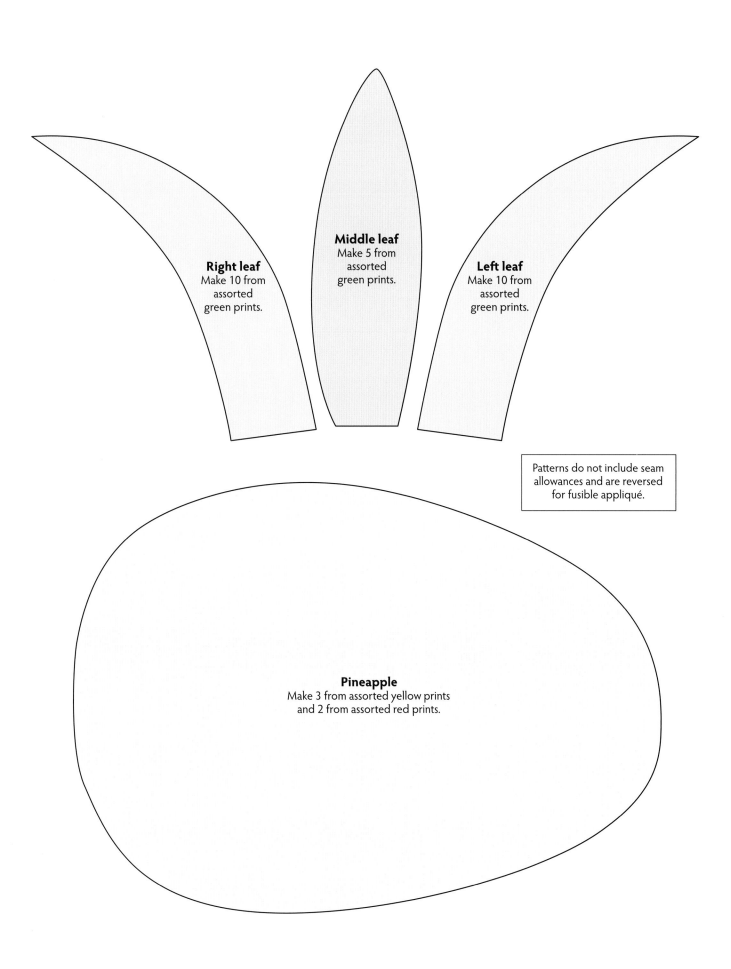

Right leaf
Make 10 from assorted green prints.

Middle leaf
Make 5 from assorted green prints.

Left leaf
Make 10 from assorted green prints.

Patterns do not include seam allowances and are reversed for fusible appliqué.

Pineapple
Make 3 from assorted yellow prints and 2 from assorted red prints.

all lined up

Free-style, wonky piecing gives this fun-to-make runner a modern look. The quilting varies in density—loose down the middle, dense in the outer pieces—which gives a nice contrast and makes the runner even more intriguing up close. » **BY TONY JACOBSON**

 Finished table runner: 19" × 48½"

materials

Yardage is based on 42"-wide fabric.

- ¼ yard *each* of 3 prints for pieced center: dark gray, turquoise, and green
- ⅞ yard of light gray print for pieced center and borders
- ¼ yard of red print for borders
- ¼ yard of teal print for borders
- ⅜ yard of green stripe for binding
- 1½ yards of fabric for backing
- 23" × 53" piece of batting
- 5" × 48" strip of freezer paper

cutting

All measurements include ¼"-wide seam allowances.

From the dark gray print, cut:
1 strip, 7" × 42"; crosscut into 12 rectangles, 2" × 7"

From the turquoise print, cut:
1 strip, 7" × 42"; crosscut into 12 rectangles, 2" × 7"
1 square, 2½" × 2½"

From the green print, cut:
1 strip, 7" × 42"; crosscut into 12 rectangles, 2" × 7"
1 square, 2½" × 2½"

From the light gray print, cut:
1 strip, 7" × 42"; crosscut into 12 rectangles, 2" × 7"
2 strips, 3" × 42"
2 strips, 2½" × 42"; crosscut into:
    1 strip, 2½" × 36½"
    3 squares, 2½" × 2½"
4 strips, 2" × 42"

From the red print, cut:
4 strips, 1" × 42"
1 square, 2½" × 2½"

From the teal print, cut:
3 strips, 2" × 42"

From the green stripe, cut:
4 strips, 2½" × 42"

making the wonky insert

1 Place a dark gray, turquoise, green, or light gray print rectangle right side up and at a slight angle on the shiny side of the freezer paper strip as shown, making sure the fabric extends at least ¼" beyond the edge of the paper. Press the strip in place with an iron to adhere the fabric to the freezer paper for a temporary hold.

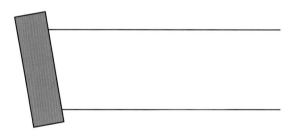

fabric arrangement

The featured runner begins with dark gray print at one end, but you can sew the pieces in any order you like. The goal is a pleasing random design.

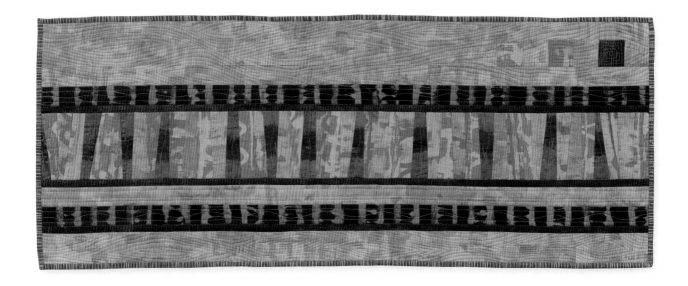

2 Place a second dark gray, turquoise, green, or light gray print rectangle right side down on top of the first rectangle, with right edges aligned. Using a ¼" seam allowance and a shortened stitch length, sew the two rectangles together on the right edges.

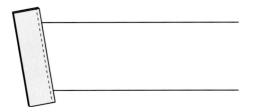

❯❯

controlling the bulk

Roll up the right end of the freezer paper and use a paper clip to hold it in place so there is less loose paper to control when sewing.

• • • • • •

3 Flip the top rectangle open and press. Take care to keep the iron on the fabric only and not on the freezer paper, as it will melt the waxy coating.

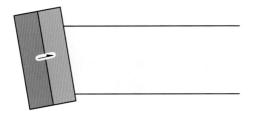

4 Place the sewn pieces on a cutting mat with the paper side up. Fold back the paper on the stitching line. Trim the second rectangle at an angle as shown. Alternate the cut angles as you proceed along the length of the freezer paper.

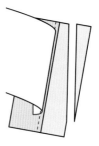

5 Unfold the paper and use an iron to adhere the second rectangle to the freezer paper to temporarily hold it in place.

6 Continue in the same manner along the length of the freezer paper until it is completely covered. (If you need additional rectangles, cut more pieces from the leftover fabrics.) There will be excess fabric around the edges of the freezer paper.

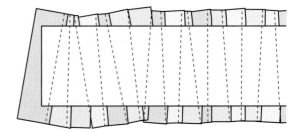

7 Using a rotary cutter and ruler, trim the excess fabric ¼" beyond the edges of the freezer paper. The wonky insert should measure 5½" × 48½", including seam allowances. Do not remove the freezer paper until you've sewn the insert into the table runner.

assembling the table-runner top

Press all seam allowances as shown by the arrows in the illustrations.

1 Sew together the light gray 2½" × 36½" strip; turquoise, green, and red squares; and three light gray squares to make a pieced row that measures 2½" × 48½", including seam allowances.

Make 1 row,
2½" × 48½".

2 Join the light gray 2"-wide strips end to end to make one long strip. From the pieced strip, cut three strips, 2" × 48½". In the same manner, join the teal 2"-wide strips end to end to make one long strip. From the pieced strip, cut two strips that measure 2" × 48½".

3 Join the red 1"-wide strips end to end to make one long strip. From the pieced strip, cut three strips, 1" × 48½". Join the light gray 3"-wide strips end to end to make one long strip. From the pieced strip, cut one strip that measures 3" × 48½".

4 Referring to the runner assembly diagram, lay out the wonky insert, pieced row, and all of the strips from steps 2–5. Join the pieces to make the table-runner top, which should measure 19" × 48½". Carefully remove the freezer paper from the back of the pieced center section.

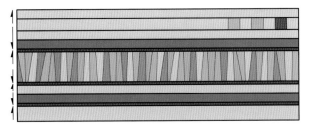

Runner assembly

finishing the table runner

For help with the following steps, find free, illustrated instructions at ShopMartingale.com/HowtoQuilt.

1 Prepare the backing so it's about 4" larger in both directions than the table-runner top. Layer the backing, batting, and table-runner top. Baste the layers together.

2 Hand or machine quilt; the runner shown is machine quilted in the outer areas with curvy lines that mimic wood grain and with straight and wavy lines in the center.

3 Use the green 2½"-wide strips to make the binding, and then attach it to the runner.

hightail

Scraps of color pop against the grayscale background in this sleek table runner. Although the triangles might appear complicated, the simple stitch-and-flip method makes them easier than they look. ›› **BY KIM LAPACEK**

›› **Finished table runner:** 12½" × 40½"

materials

Yardage is based on 42"-wide fabric. Fat quarters measure 18" × 21".

- 4 fat quarters, 1 *each* of pale, light, medium, and dark gray print for background

- 10 squares, 10" × 10", of assorted prints for flying-geese units and half-square-triangle units: dark red, red, orange, amber, yellow, green, turquoise, blue, purple, and magenta

- ¼ yard of multicolored stripe for binding

- 1 yard of fabric for backing

- 17" × 45" piece of batting

cutting

Refer to the photo for color placement or do your own thing! Choose your colors for the flying-geese and half-square-triangle units as you assemble each section. Letters in parentheses refer to the sections in which the gray pieces are used. As you cut, separate the gray pieces into their respective sections, A–J.

All measurements include ¼"-wide seam allowances.

From the pale gray print, cut:

1 strip, 3½" × 21"; crosscut into:
    1 rectangle, 3½" × 5½" (J)
    1 square, 3½" × 3½" (H)
    1 rectangle, 2½" × 3½" (A)
2 strips, 2½" × 21"; crosscut into:
    1 strip, 2½" × 13½" (A)
    3 squares, 2½" × 2½" (A, F, and H)
    1 rectangle, 2½" × 6½" (F)

3 strips, 1½" × 21"; crosscut into:
    1 strip, 1½" × 16½" (A)
    1 strip, 1½" × 8½" (F)
    1 rectangle, 1½" × 6½" (H)
    1 rectangle, 1½" × 4½" (H)
    1 rectangle, 1½" × 2½" (H)
    4 squares, 1½" × 1½" (*2 each* for A and H)

From the light gray print, cut:

1 strip, 3½" × 21"; crosscut into:
    4 squares, 3½" × 3½" (*1 each* for C and H; 2 for F)
    1 rectangle, 1½" × 3½" (D)
2 strips, 2½" × 21"; crosscut into:
    2 rectangles, 2½" × 4½" (B and E)
    1 rectangle, 2½" × 3½" (H)
    7 squares, 2½" × 2½" (2 for H; *1 each* for C, D, E, F, and J)
2 strips, 1½" × 21"; crosscut into:
    1 rectangle, 1½" × 5½" (J)
    9 rectangles, 1½" × 2½" (*1 each* for B, C, D, F, and H; *2 each* for E and J)
    8 squares, 1½" × 1½" (*2 each* for B, E, H, and J)

From the medium gray print, cut:

2 strips, 3½" × 21"; crosscut into:
    2 squares, 3½" × 3½" (C and F)
    5 rectangles, 2½" × 3½" (*1 each* for B, C, and F; 2 for I)
1 strip, 2½" × 21"; crosscut into 8 squares, 2½" × 2½" (*1 each* for B, D, E, and F; *2 each* for I and J)
3 strips, 1½" × 21"; crosscut into:
    1 rectangle, 1½" × 6½" (E)
    1 rectangle, 1½" × 4½" (I)
    3 rectangles, 1½" × 3½" (D, E, and J)
    6 rectangles, 1½" × 2½" (*1 each* for D, E, I, and J; 2 for F)
    9 squares, 1½" × 1½" (3 for E; *2 each* for B and J; *1 each* for F and I)

Continued on page 24

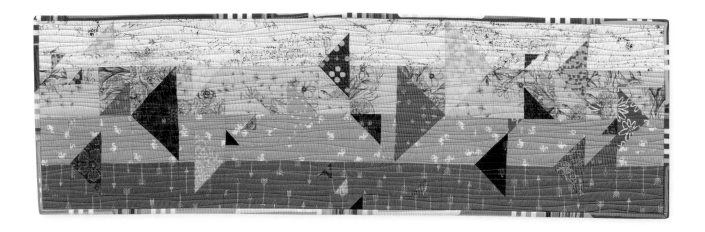

Continued from page 23

From the dark gray print, cut:

2 strips, 3½" × 21"; crosscut into:
  1 rectangle, 3½" × 6½" (E)
  2 rectangles, 3½" × 5½" (C and J)
  2 rectangles, 2½" × 3½" (I)
1 strip, 2½" × 21"; crosscut into:
  5 squares, 2½" × 2½" (*2 each* for B and I; 1 for D)
  2 rectangles, 1½" × 2½" (D and G)
2 strips, 1½" × 21"; crosscut into:
  2 rectangles, 1½" × 7½" (G and I)
  1 rectangle, 1½" × 5½" (G)
  2 rectangles, 1½" × 4½" (B and G)
  1 rectangle, 1½" × 3½" (D)
  6 squares, 1½" × 1½" (G)

From the assorted print squares, cut a *total* of:

3 rectangles, 3½" × 6½"
8 rectangles, 2½" × 4½"
6 squares, 2½" × 2½"
16 squares, 1½" × 1½"

From the multicolored stripe, cut:

3 strips, 2½" × 42"

making the flying-geese and half-square-triangle units

Using the following instructions, make flying-geese units and half-square-triangle units as you assemble each section, referring to the diagrams and photo for correct placement of the gray pieces. Press all seam allowances as shown by the arrows in the illustrations.

flying-geese units

1 Draw a diagonal line from corner to corner on the wrong side of the appropriate gray 3½" squares. Place a marked square on one end of a print 3½" × 6½" rectangle, right sides together. Stitch on the line; trim away the excess fabric, leaving a ¼" seam allowance; press.

2 Repeat on the opposite end of the rectangle with another 3½" square. Stitch, trim, and press to complete a flying-geese unit that measures 3½" × 6½", including seam allowances.

Make 1 unit,
3½" × 6½".

3 In the same manner, make 2½" × 4½" flying-geese units using print 2½" × 4½" rectangles and gray 2½" squares.

Make 1 unit,
2½" × 4½".

half-square-triangle units

To make a 2½" half-square-triangle unit, draw a diagonal line from corner to corner on the wrong side of a gray 2½" square. Place the square on a print 2½" square, right sides together. Sew on the drawn line. Cut ¼" from the line *on one side only*. The half-square-triangle unit should measure 2½" square. Discard the two triangles. In the same manner, make a 1½" half-square-triangle unit using print and gray 1½" squares.

Make 1 unit,   Make 1 unit,
2½" × 2½".   1½" × 1½".

assembling the sections

For each section, lay out the pieces according to the assembly diagrams. When assembling, first join the smallest pieces in pairs or rows, and then add the next larger pieces. Press all seam allowances as shown by the arrows.

1 Using pieces cut for section A, make a 2½" half-square-triangle unit and a 1½" half-square-triangle unit. Lay out the units and the remaining pale gray A pieces. Join the pieces to make section A, which should measure 3½" × 18½", including seam allowances.

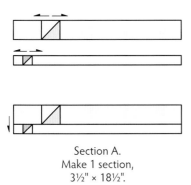

Section A.
Make 1 section,
3½" × 18½".

2 Using pieces cut for section B, make a 2½" × 4½" flying-geese unit and two 1½" half-square-triangle units. Lay out the units and the remaining light, medium, and dark gray B pieces. Join the pieces to make section B, which should measure 4½" × 9½", including seam allowances.

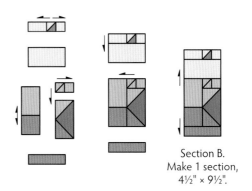

Section B.
Make 1 section,
4½" × 9½".

3 Using pieces cut for section C, make a 3½" × 6½" flying-geese unit and a 2½" half-square-triangle unit. Lay out the units and the remaining light, medium, and dark gray C pieces. Join the pieces to make section C, which should measure 5½" × 9½", including seam allowances.

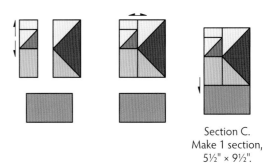

Section C.
Make 1 section,
5½" × 9½".

4 Using pieces cut for section D, make a 2½" × 4½" flying-geese unit and a 2½" half-square-triangle unit. Lay out the units and the remaining light, medium, and dark gray D pieces. Join the pieces to make section D, which should measure 3½" × 9½", including seam allowances.

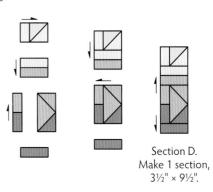

Section D.
Make 1 section,
3½" × 9½".

5 Using pieces cut for section E, make a 2½" × 4½" flying-geese unit and three 1½" half-square-triangle units. Lay out the units and the remaining light, medium, and dark gray E pieces. Join the pieces to make section E, which should measure 6½" × 9½", including seam allowances.

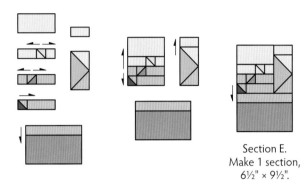

Section E.
Make 1 section,
6½" × 9½".

6 Using pieces cut for section F, make a 3½" × 6½" flying-geese unit, a 2½" × 4½" flying-geese unit, a 2½" half-square-triangle unit, and a 1½" half-square-triangle unit. Lay out the units and the remaining pale, light, and medium gray F pieces. Join the pieces to make section F, which should measure 8½" × 9½", including seam allowances.

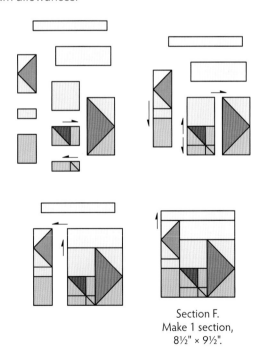

Section F.
Make 1 section,
8½" × 9½".

protect your fingers!

Use a stiletto to hold the nested seams together as you sew. The stiletto's point can get closer to the needle than your fingers should!

. . . . . .

7 Using pieces cut for section G, make four 1½" half-square-triangle units. Lay out the units and the remaining dark gray G pieces. Join the pieces to make section G, which should measure 3½" × 8½", including seam allowances.

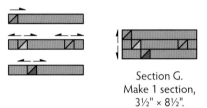

Section G.
Make 1 section,
3½" × 8½".

8 Using pieces cut for section H, make a 3½" × 6½" flying-geese unit, a 2½" × 4½" flying-geese unit, a 2½" half-square-triangle unit, and two 1½" half-square-triangle units. Lay out the units and the remaining pale and light gray H pieces. Join the pieces to make section H, which should measure 6½" × 9½", including seam allowances.

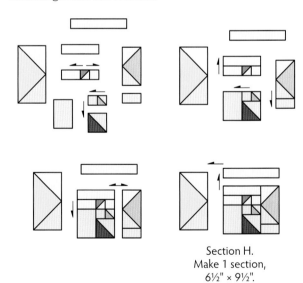

Section H.
Make 1 section,
6½" × 9½".

9 Using pieces cut for section I, make two 2½" × 4½" flying-geese units and a 1½" half-square-triangle unit. Lay out the units and the remaining medium and dark gray I pieces. Join the pieces to make section I, which should measure 6½" × 9½", including seam allowances.

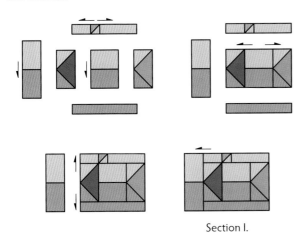

Section I.
Make 1 section,
6½" × 9½".

10 Using pieces cut for section J, make a 2½" × 4½" flying-geese unit, a 2½" half-square-triangle unit, and two 1½" half-square-triangle units. Lay out the units and the remaining pale, light, medium, and dark gray J pieces. Join the pieces to make section J, which should measure 5½" × 12½", including seam allowances.

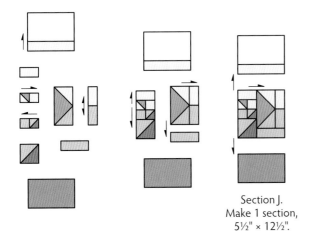

Section J.
Make 1 section,
5½" × 12½".

assembling the table-runner top

1 Referring to the runner assembly diagram, lay out sections A–J. Join sections B, C, D, and E. Add section A.

2 Join sections F and G. Join sections H and I, and then join all of the units to complete the table-runner top. The top should measure 12½" × 40½".

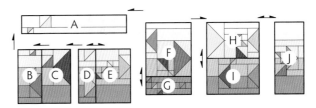

Runner assembly

finishing the table runner

For help with the following steps, find free, illustrated instructions at ShopMartingale.com/HowtoQuilt.

1 Prepare the backing so it's about 4" larger in both directions than the table-runner top. Layer the backing, batting, and table-runner top. Baste the layers together.

2 Hand or machine quilt; the runner shown is machine quilted with slightly curving lines spaced ¼" to ½" apart along the length of the runner.

3 Use the multicolored 2½"-wide strips to make the binding, and then attach it to the runner.

farm fresh

Create a warm and welcoming accent piece for your farmhouse table. The design density varies from one fabric to the next—from small- to large-scale prints—and gives extra sparkle to the stars that float in these asymmetrical Log Cabin blocks. » **BY SUE PFAU**

» **Finished table runner:** 19½" × 45"
Finished block: 8½" × 8½"

materials

Yardage is based on 42"-wide fabric. Fat quarters measure 18"×21".

- 10 fat quarters of assorted medium to dark prints for blocks and border (collectively referred to as *dark*)
- ½ yard of cream print for background
- ⅜ yard of blue print for binding
- 1⅜ yards of fabric for backing
- 24" × 49" piece of batting

cutting

All measurements include ¼"-wide seam allowances.

From *each* dark print, cut:
1 strip, 1½" × 21"; crosscut into 2 strips, 1½" × 9" (20 total; 6 are extra)
3 strips, 1¾" × 21"; crosscut into:
    1 strip, 1¾" × 9" (10 total)
    2 strips, 1¾" × 7¾" (20 total)
    1 strip, 1¾" × 6½" (10 total)
8 squares, 1¾" × 1¾" (80 total)
1 square, 3" × 3" (10 total)

From the remainder of *1* dark print, cut:
4 squares, 1½" × 1½"

From the cream print, cut:
6 strips, 2¼" × 42"; crosscut into:
    40 rectangles, 2¼" × 3"
    40 squares, 2¼" × 2¼"

From the blue print, cut:
4 strips, 2½" × 42"

making the blocks

Press all seam allowances as shown by the arrows in the illustrations.

1   Draw a diagonal line from corner to corner on the wrong side of eight matching dark 1¾" squares. Place a marked square on one end of a cream 2¼" × 3" rectangle, right sides together. Sew on the line, and then trim ¼" from the stitching; press.

2   Repeat to sew a second marked square to the opposite end of the rectangle from step 1 to make a star-point unit. Make four matching star-point units that measure 2¼" × 3", including seam allowances.

Make 4 units,
2¼" × 3".

3   Repeat steps 1 and 2 to make 10 sets of four matching star-point units (40 total).

4 Arrange four cream 2¼" squares, four matching star-point units, and a matching dark 3" square in three rows as shown. Sew the pieces together in each row. Join the rows to make a star unit. Make 10 star units that measure 6½" square, including seam allowances.

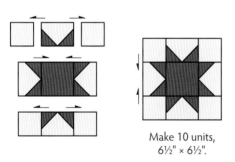

Make 10 units,
6½" × 6½".

5 Sew a dark 1¾" × 6½" strip to the top of a star unit. Then add a different dark 1¾" × 7¾" strip to the left edge.

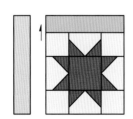 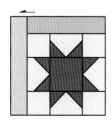

6 Sew a dark 1¾" × 7¾" strip to the top of the star unit. Then add a different dark 1¾" × 9" strip to the left edge to complete a block. Repeat to make a total of 10 blocks that measure 9" square, including seam allowances.

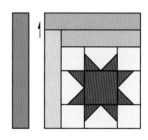 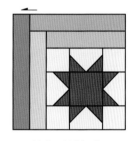

Make 10 blocks,
9" × 9".

color arrangement

Arrange the star units on a design wall. Place strips around them, rearranging until you like the color balance, and then sew the strips to the star units.

......

assembling the table-runner top

1 Lay out the blocks in two horizontal rows, rotating the blocks as shown. Join the blocks in each row, and then join the rows to make the table-runner center. The table-runner center should measure 17½" × 43", including seam allowances.

Runner assembly

2 Arrange five assorted dark 1½" × 9" strips along each side of the quilt center and two strips along each end. When you are satisfied with the color arrangement, sew the strips together end to end to make two long borders and two short borders.

3 Sew the long borders to the sides of the table-runner center. Sew a 1½" square to each end of the short borders, and add the borders to the ends of the table-runner center. The table-runner top should measure 19½" × 45".

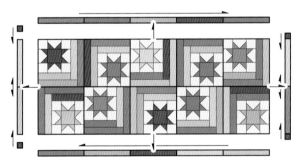

Adding borders

scrappy borders

You will have plenty of leftover fabric if you need to cut more pieces for the borders. Sometimes the fabrics you have left at the end aren't quite right, or you want to add more of a favorite color or print.

· · · · · ·

finishing the table runner

For help with the following steps, find free, illustrated instructions at ShopMartingale.com/HowtoQuilt.

1 Prepare the backing so it's about 4" larger in both directions than the table-runner top. Layer the backing, batting, and table-runner top. Baste the layers together.

2 Hand or machine quilt; the runner shown is machine quilted with an allover feather design.

3 Use the blue 2½"-wide strips to make the binding, and then attach it to the runner.

The blue print is larger in scale than the cream print, adding dimension to this block.

improv under control

Love the look of improvisational patchwork but not sure where to start? Follow the pattern as specified or take the opportunity to make it your own! » **BY MIRANDA ROSA**

» **Finished table runner:** 14½" × 42½"
Finished block: 14" × 14"

materials

Yardage is based on 42"-wide fabric.

- ⅛ yard *each* of 5 batiks for blocks: purple, blue, yellow, pink, and teal
- ¼ yard *each* of 3 batiks for blocks: black, green, and orange
- ½ yard of tangerine batik for blocks and binding
- 1⅜ yards of fabric for backing
- 19" × 47" piece of batting

cutting

All measurements include ¼"-wide seam allowances.

From the purple batik, cut:
1 strip, 2½" × 42"; crosscut into:
    1 strip, 2½" × 14½"
    1 strip, 2½" × 12½"
    1 square, 2½" × 2½"

From the blue batik, cut:
1 strip, 2½" × 42"; crosscut into:
    2 rectangles, 2½" × 4½"
    2 squares, 2½" × 2½"

From the black batik, cut:
2 strips, 2½" × 42"; crosscut into:
    2 strips, 2½" × 10½"
    1 strip, 2½" × 8½"
    2 strips, 2½" × 6½"
    2 rectangles, 2½" × 4½"

From the yellow batik, cut:
1 strip, 2½" × 42"; crosscut into:
    2 strips, 2½" × 8½"
    2 strips, 2½" × 6½"
    1 square, 2½" × 2½"

From the tangerine batik cut:
5 strips, 2½" × 42"; crosscut *1 of the strips* into:
    1 strip, 2½" × 10½"
    2 strips, 2½" × 8½"
    1 strip, 2½" × 6½"

From the green batik, cut:
2 strips, 2½" × 42"; crosscut into:
    3 strips, 2½" × 12½"
    3 strips, 2½" × 10½"

From the orange batik, cut:
2 strips, 2½" × 42"; crosscut into:
    2 strips, 2½" × 14½"
    1 strip, 2½" × 12½"
    1 square, 2½" × 2½"

From the pink batik, cut:
1 strip, 2½" × 42"; crosscut into:
    1 strip, 2½" × 6½"
    2 rectangles, 2½" × 4½"
    1 square, 2½" × 2½"

From the teal batik, cut:
1 strip, 2½" × 42"; crosscut into:
    1 strip, 2½" × 12½"
    1 strip, 2½" × 8½"

From the remainders of all batiks, cut:
18–22 strips, 2½"-wide × random lengths varying from 1" to 2½"

making the blocks

This quilt is assembled Log Cabin–style with assorted batik scraps inserted into some of the strips before they're added to the block center. Press all seam allowances as shown by the arrows in the illustrations.

1 Sew together the purple 2½" square and a blue 2½" square. Add a blue 2½" × 4½" rectangle to the left of the pieced unit to make a center unit that measures 4½" square, including seam allowances.

Make 1 unit,
4½" × 4½".

2 Add a black 2½" × 4½" rectangle to the right of the block center and a black 2½" × 6½" strip to the bottom edge, completing the first round of Log Cabin strips. The unit should measure 6½" square, including seam allowances.

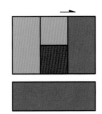 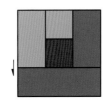

Make 1 unit,
6½" × 6½".

3 Cut a yellow 2½" × 6½" strip crosswise, at least 1" from one end. Insert one, two, or three 2½"-wide scraps cut from the remainders of the batiks. Trim the pieced yellow strip to 6½" in length. Add the fabric you cut off the strip to your batik scrap pile.

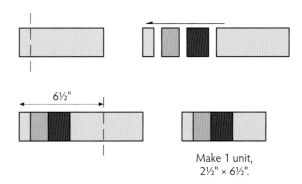

6½"

Make 1 unit,
2½" × 6½".

4 Sew the pieced yellow strip from step 3 to the top edge of the block center. The unit should measure 6½" × 8½".

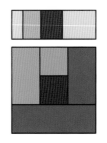 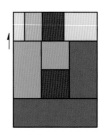

Make 1 unit,
6½" × 8½".

5 Repeat step 3, inserting scraps into a yellow 2½" × 8½" strip to make a pieced strip. Trim the strip to 8½" long. Sew the strip to the left edge of the block center. The unit should measure 8½" square, including seam allowances.

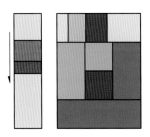 

Make 1 unit,
8½" × 8½".

6 To add the third round of strips, add a tangerine 2½" × 8½" strip to the right of the block center, the tangerine 2½" × 10½" strip to the bottom edge, the green 2½" × 10½" strip to the top edge, and a green 2½" × 12½" strip to the left edge. The unit should measure 12½" square, including seam allowances.

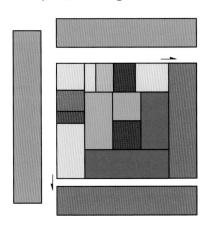

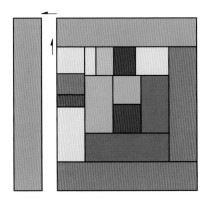

Make 1 unit,
12½" × 12½".

7 Repeat step 3 using the purple 2½" × 12½" and 2½" × 14½" strips. Sew the pieced purple strips to the right and bottom edges of the block center to complete block A. The block should measure 14½" square, including seam allowances.

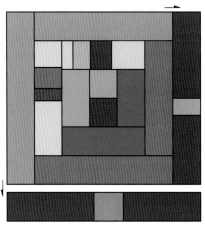

Block A.
Make 1 block,
14½" × 14½".

8 For block B, gather the following pieces:
- 1 orange 2½" square
- 1 orange 2½" × 12½" strip
- 1 orange 2½" × 14½" strip
- 1 pink 2½" square
- 1 pink 2½" × 4½" rectangle
- 1 black 2½" × 4½" rectangle
- 1 black 2½" × 6½" strip
- 1 yellow 2½" × 6½" strip
- 1 yellow 2½" × 8½" strip
- 1 teal 2½" × 8½" strip
- 1 teal 2½" × 12½" strip
- 2 green 2½" × 10½" strips

make it your own!

Make this project your own by adding fabric scraps in different spots! There are no rules about where the scraps need to be inserted or how many to add. Just make sure that once you've inserted the scraps, you trim the pieced strip to fit the Log Cabin block.

· · · · · · ·

9 Using the gathered pieces and referring to the diagram, make a block center, and then add strips Log Cabin–style to the block center, inserting scraps into the strips as desired.

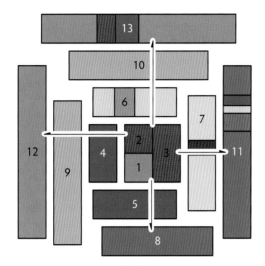

Block B.
Make 1 block,
14½" × 14½".

10 For block C, gather the following pieces:
- 1 yellow 2½" square
- 1 blue 2½" square
- 1 blue 2½" × 4½" rectangle
- 1 pink 2½" × 4½" rectangle
- 1 pink 2½" × 6½" strip
- 1 tangerine 2½" × 6½" strip
- 1 tangerine 2½" × 8½" strip
- 1 black 2½" × 8½" strip
- 2 black 2½" × 10½" strips
- 2 green 2½" × 12½" strips
- 1 orange 2½" × 14½" strip

11 Using the gathered strips and referring to the diagram, make a block center, and then add strips Log Cabin–style to the block center, inserting scraps into the strips as desired.

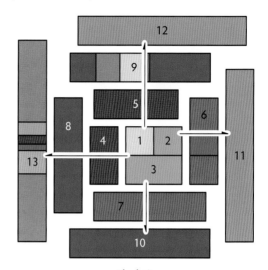

Block C.
Make 1 block,
14½" × 14½".

assembling the table-runner top

Join the three blocks into a row to make the table-runner top, which should measure 14½" × 42½".

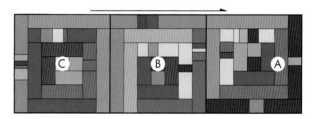

Runner assembly

finishing the table runner

For help with the following steps, find free, illustrated instructions at ShopMartingale.com/HowtoQuilt.

1 Prepare the backing so it's about 4" larger in both directions than the table-runner top. Layer the backing, batting, and table-runner top. Baste the layers together.

2 Hand or machine quilt; the runner shown is machine quilted with an allover stipple.

3 Use the tangerine 2½"-wide strips to make the binding, and then attach it to the runner.

making waves

What a fun way to introduce the illusion of curves! The floating squares in this unusual runner add rhythmic movement to blocks created from simple pieced bars. Narrow navy lines offset the colorful stripes, creating drama and balancing the design. » **BY JULIE TAYLOR**

» **Finished table runner:** 18½" × 51½"
Finished block: 17" × 18"

materials

Yardage is based on 42"-wide fabric.

- 1 yard of light gray print for background

- 6 strips, 1½" × 42", of assorted gray, blue, turquoise, aqua, and yellow prints for blocks*

- ½ yard of navy solid for blocks and binding

- 1⅝ yards of fabric for backing

- 23" × 56" piece of batting

After removing the selvage ends, measure the strips to make sure they're at least 42" long. If not, you may need to cut additional strips.

cutting

All measurements include ¼"-wide seam allowances.

From the light gray print, cut:
2 strips, 5½" × 42"; crosscut into 3 rectangles,
    5½" × 17½"
14 strips, 1½" × 42"; crosscut into:
    3 strips, 1½" × 17½"
    27 strips, 1½" × 12½"
    6 rectangles, 1½" × 3½"
    6 rectangles, 1½" × 2½"
    42 squares, 1½" × 1½"

From each of 3 print strips, cut:
1 strip, 1½" × 9½" (3 total)
1 strip, 1½" × 8½" (3 total)
1 strip, 1½" × 7½" (3 total)
1 strip, 1½" × 6½" (3 total)
4 squares, 1½" × 1½" (12 total)

From each of the 3 remaining print strips, cut:
1 strip, 1½" × 10½" (3 total)
1 strip, 1½" × 9½" (3 total)
1 strip, 1½" × 8½" (3 total)
1 strip, 1½" × 7½" (3 total)
4 squares, 1½" × 1½" (12 total)

From the navy solid, cut:
3 strips, 1" × 17½"
4 strips, 2" × 42"*

Julie used 2"-wide binding strips. If you prefer to cut yours 2½" wide, you'll have sufficient yardage to do so.

making the color bars

All pieced bars in steps 1–8 should measure 1½" × 12½", including seam allowances. Press all seam allowances as shown by the arrows in the illustrations.

1 Sew together two light gray 1½" squares, a print 1½" × 6½" strip, a matching print 1½" square, and a light gray 1½" × 3½" rectangle as shown to make bar A. Repeat to make a total of three A bars.

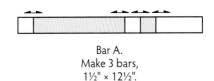

Bar A.
Make 3 bars,
1½" × 12½".

assembly tip

If you are using directional fabric, make sure the print fabric squares follow the same direction as the rectangles when assembling the bars.

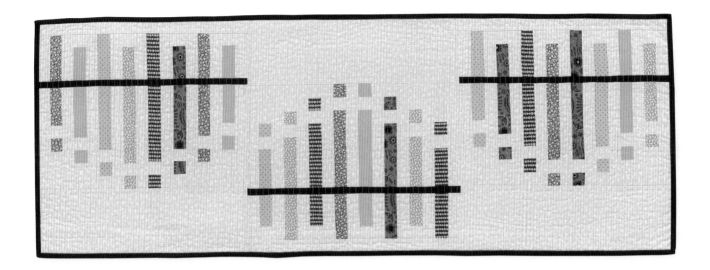

2 Join a print 1½" × 8½" strip, a matching print 1½" square, a light gray 1½" square, and a light gray 1½" × 2½" rectangle as shown to make bar B. Repeat to make a total of three B bars.

Bar B.
Make 3 bars,
1½" × 12½".

3 Sew together three light gray 1½" squares, a print 1½" × 8½" strip, and a matching print 1½" square as shown to make bar C. Repeat to make a total of three C bars.

Bar C.
Make 3 bars,
1½" × 12½".

4 Join a print 1½" × 10½" strip, a matching print 1½" square, and a light gray 1½" square as shown to make bar D. Repeat to make a total of three D bars.

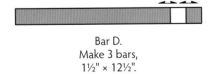

Bar D.
Make 3 bars,
1½" × 12½".

5 Sew together two light gray 1½" squares, a print 1½" × 9½" strip, and a matching print 1½" square as shown to make bar E. Repeat to make a total of three E bars.

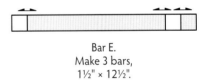

Bar E.
Make 3 bars,
1½" × 12½".

6 Join a print 1½" × 9½" strip, a matching print 1½" square, and two light gray 1½" squares as shown to make bar F. Repeat to make a total of three F bars.

Bar F.
Make 3 bars,
1½" × 12½".

7 Sew together two light gray 1½" squares, a light gray 1½" × 2½" rectangle, a print 1½" × 7½" strip, and a matching print 1½" square as shown to make bar G. Repeat to make a total of three G bars.

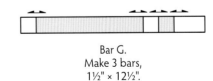

Bar G.
Make 3 bars,
1½" × 12½".

8 Join a print 1½" × 7½" strip, a matching print 1½" square, a light gray 1½" square, and a light gray 1½" × 3½" rectangle as shown to make bar H. Repeat to make a total of three H bars.

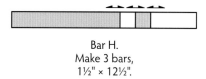

Bar H.
Make 3 bars,
1½" × 12½".

making the blocks

1 Sew together nine light gray 1½" × 12½" strips alternating with one *each* of bars A through H. The unit should measure 12½" × 17½", including seam allowances.

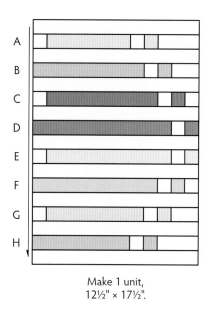

Make 1 unit,
12½" × 17½".

keep it straight

When sewing strips and bars together, alternate the sewing direction from seam to seam to help prevent distortion in the finished piece.

• • • • • •

2 Using a ruler and rotary cutter, cut vertically through the unit, 4" from the left edge. Sew a navy 1" × 17½" strip between the two pieces. The unit should measure 12½" × 17½".

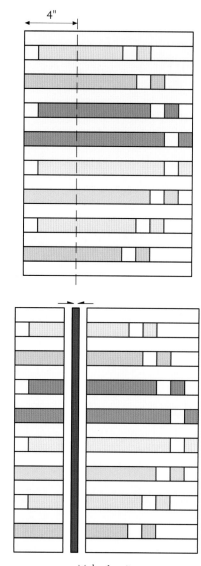

Make 1 unit,
12½" × 17½".

3 Sew a light gray 1½" × 17½" strip to the left edge of the unit and a light gray 5½" × 17½" rectangle to the right edge to make a block that measures 18½" × 17½", including seam allowances.

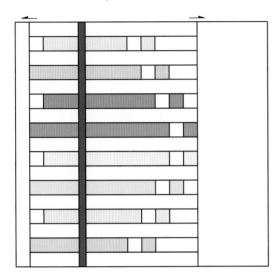

Make 3 blocks,
18½" × 17½".

4 Repeat steps 1–3 to make a total of three blocks.

assembling the table-runner top

Referring to the photo on page 39 and the illustration below, lay out the three blocks, rotating the middle block 180°. Join the blocks to make the table-runner top, which should measure 18½" × 51½".

finishing the table runner

For help with the following steps, find free, illustrated instructions at ShopMartingale.com/HowtoQuilt.

1 Prepare the backing so it's about 4" larger in both directions than the table-runner top. Layer the backing, batting, and table-runner top. Baste the layers together.

2 Hand or machine quilt; the runner shown is machine quilted with horizontal lines across the width, ¼" from each seam.

3 Use the navy 2"-wide strips to make the binding, and then attach it to the runner.

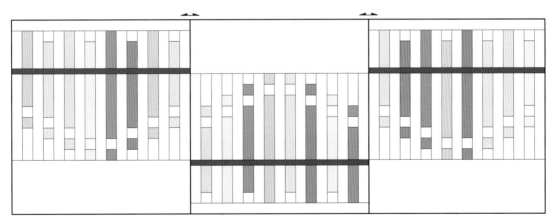

Runner assembly

star-in-a-star

Table mats add a handmade touch underneath plant pots, vases, and candles, or as a centerpiece on the dining table. To make this design for different seasons, consider yellows for spring, gorgeous russets for fall, or festive fabrics to adorn your holiday table. » **BY JULIE TAYLOR**

» **Finished table mat:** 23½" from point to point
Finished block: 4" × 4"

materials

Yardage is based on 42"-wide fabric. Fat quarters measure 18" × 21". Fat eighths measure 9" × 21".

- 1 fat quarter of light print for block backgrounds
- 1 fat eighth of light gray print for blocks
- 1 fat eighth of dark gray solid for blocks
- ¾ yard of red print for blocks, pieced triangles, and binding
- ⅞ yard of fabric for backing
- 28" × 28" square of batting

cutting

All measurements include ¼"-wide seam allowances.

From the light print, cut:
1 strip, 3" × 21"; crosscut into 6 squares, 3" × 3"
3 strips, 2½" × 21"; crosscut into 24 squares, 2½" × 2½"

From the light gray print, cut:
1 strip, 3" × 21"; crosscut into 6 squares, 3" × 3"

From the dark gray solid, cut:
1 strip, 4½" × 21"; crosscut into 4 squares, 4½" × 4½"

From the red print, cut:
2"-wide bias strips totaling 90" when joined for binding

From the remainder of the red print, cut:
20 squares, 4½" × 4½"

making the blocks

Press all seam allowances as shown by the arrows in the illustrations.

1 Draw a diagonal line from corner to corner on the wrong side of each light print 3" square. Place a marked square on a light gray 3" square, right sides together. Sew ¼" from both sides of the line. Cut on the drawn line to yield two half-square-triangle units. Trim the units to 2½" square. Repeat to make a total of 12 half-square-triangle units.

Make 12 units.

2 Sew two light print 2½" squares to the gray sides of a half-square-triangle unit as shown. Repeat to make a total of 12 units.

Make 12 units.

3 Draw a diagonal line from corner to corner on the wrong side of each unit from step 2 as shown. The line should pass through the seam intersection.

4 Place a marked unit from step 3 on a dark gray 4½" square, right sides together. Stitch on the drawn line. Trim ¼" from the drawn line as shown. Open the unit and press. Repeat to make a total of four blocks that measure 4½" square, including seam allowances.

Make 4 blocks,
4½" × 4½".

5 Repeat step 4 to make eight blocks, using red 4½" squares instead of dark gray squares.

Make 8 blocks,
4½" × 4½".

assembling the table-mat top

1 Arrange four red 4½" squares, four gray blocks, and eight red blocks in four rows, rotating them as shown. Join the pieces in each row. Join the rows to make a large star, which should measure 16½" square, including seam allowances.

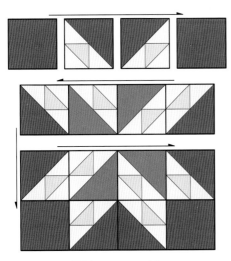

Table-mat assembly

2 Draw a diagonal line from corner to corner on the wrong side of four red 4½" squares. Place a marked square on an unmarked red 4½" square, right sides together. Sew one edge as shown, and then trim ¼" from the diagonal line. Repeat to make four pieced triangles.

Sew.

¼"

Make 4 pieced triangles.

handling star points

The red print pieced triangles have bias edges. Handle and press with care to prevent stretching and distortion.

· · · · · ·

3 Position a pieced triangle in the center of each star edge, matching the center seams. Sew the pieced triangles to the star, beginning and ending the seams ¼" from the edge of the pieced triangle (the stitching should end exactly on the seamline where the rows join). Press the points of the triangle at the ends of the stitching toward the wrong side before pressing the seam allowances away from the center of the mat.

Adding triangles.

finishing the table mat

For help with the following steps, find free, illustrated instructions at ShopMartingale.com/HowtoQuilt.

1 Prepare the backing so it's about 4" larger in both directions than the table-mat top. Layer the backing, batting, and table-mat top. Baste the layers together.

2 Hand or machine quilt; the table mat shown is machine quilted with two V shapes in each block and pieced triangle.

3 Stay-stitch around the edge of the mat a scant ¼" from the edge. Carefully snip into the inside corners, stopping just before the stay stitching.

4 Use the red 2"-wide bias strips to make the binding. Attach it to the mat, proceeding as follows when you come to an inside corner: Stop at the center of the corner with the needle down. Lift the presser foot and pull the edge of the mat straight (the small cut into the corner allows you to do this). Put the presser foot down and continue to sew, holding any folds in the mat away from the presser foot, so they don't get caught. Once you have finished attaching the binding, carefully cut a V through all three layers into the seam allowance at each inner corner, ensuring that you don't cut into the seam itself. Slip-stitch the binding to the back.

moving along

Combine two traditional blocks and use fabrics with strong contrast for maximum impact in this off-center design. Quilted arcs in the Square-in-a-Square blocks suggest the much more complicated Cathedral Window design. » **BY TONY JACOBSON**

» **Finished table runner:** 16½" × 36½"

materials

Yardage is based on 42"-wide fabric.

- ⅜ yard of blue stripe for flying-geese units
- ⅓ yard of blue print for flying-geese units
- ⅞ yard of brown print for blocks and binding
- ⅝ yard of tan print for blocks
- ⅝ yard of fabric for backing
- 21" × 41" piece of batting

cutting

All measurements include ¼"-wide seam allowances.

From the blue stripe, cut:
3 strips, 2½" × 42"; crosscut into 44 squares, 2½" × 2½"
1 square, 4½" × 4½"

From the blue print, cut:
2 strips, 4½" × 42"; crosscut into 22 rectangles, 2½" × 4½"

From the brown print, cut:
2 strips, 4½" × 42"; crosscut into 12 squares, 4½" × 4½"
6 strips, 2½" × 42"; crosscut *3 of the strips* into 48
    squares, 2½" × 2½"

From the tan print, cut:
2 strips, 4½" × 42"; crosscut into 12 squares, 4½" × 4½"
3 strips, 2½" × 42"; crosscut into 48 squares, 2½" × 2½"

making the flying-geese units

Press all seam allowances as shown by the arrows in the illustrations.

1 Lay out six stripe 2½" squares, wrong side up, with stripes running horizontally. Draw a diagonal line from the lower-left to the upper-right corner on the wrong side of each square. Draw a second line ½" from the first line as shown. Lay out six more stripe 2½" squares, again with stripes running horizontally, and mark diagonal lines in the *opposite* direction.

Mark 6 of each unit
with horizontal stripes.

2 Lay out 16 stripe 2½" squares, wrong side up, with stripes running *vertically*. On the wrong side of each square, draw a diagonal line from the lower-left to the upper-right corner. Draw a second line ½" from the first line as shown. Lay out the remaining 16 stripe 2½" squares, again with stripes running vertically, and mark the diagonal lines in the *opposite* direction.

Mark 16 of each unit
with vertical stripes.

3 Place a marked stripe square from step 1 on a blue print rectangle, right sides together, as shown, making sure the second line is closest to the outer corner. Stitch on both drawn lines. Cut between the stitching lines; press. Place another marked stripe square from step 1 on the other end of the blue print rectangle. Stitch on the drawn lines. Cut between the stitching lines. Press open to complete one flying-geese unit that measures 2½" × 4½", plus two bonus half-square-triangle units. Repeat to make a total of six flying-geese units with vertical stripes.

Make 6 units,
2½" × 4½".

pay attention when piecing

The design of the table runner has the blue stripes going the same direction throughout the runner. Pay close attention to how the lines on the back of the squares are marked. You will need the correct number for each flying-geese unit to keep the stripes going in the same direction.

• • • • • •

4 Using marked stripe squares from step 2, repeat step 3 to make 16 flying-geese units with horizontal stripes.

Make 16 units,
2½" × 4½".

making the square-in-a-square units

1 On the wrong side of each brown and tan 2½" square, draw a diagonal line from corner to corner. Draw a second line ½" from the first line as shown.

Mark 48 of each unit.

2 Place a marked brown square on one corner of a tan 4½" square, right sides together, as shown. Stitch on both marked lines, and then cut between the two sewn lines. Stitch a marked brown square to each remaining corner of the tan square to make a square-in-a-square unit. (You'll have four bonus half-square-triangle units for another project. See "Waste Not, Want Not!" below right.) Repeat to make 12 tan square-in-a-square units that measure 4½" square.

Make 12 units,
4½" × 4½".

3 Using marked tan squares and brown 4½" squares, make 12 brown square-in-a-square units.

Make 12 units,
4½" × 4½".

assembling the table-runner top

Lay out the flying-geese units, square-in-a-square units, and a stripe 4½" square in four rows as shown. Sew together the pieces in each row. Join the rows to make the table-runner top, which should measure 16½" × 36½".

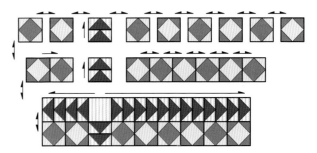

Runner assembly

finishing the table runner

For help with the following steps, find free, illustrated instructions at ShopMartingale.com/HowtoQuilt.

1 Prepare the backing so it's about 4" larger in both directions than the table-runner top. Layer the backing, batting, and table-runner top. Baste the layers together.

2 Hand or machine quilt; the runner shown is machine quilted with arcs from corner to corner in the Square-in-a-Square blocks and with straight lines ¼" from the seams in the Flying Geese blocks.

3 Use the brown 2½"-wide strips to make the binding, and then attach it to the runner.

waste not, want not!

Use the extra half-square-triangle units you've made to create mug mats that coordinate with your table runner. Experiment with different layouts to create a variety of designs. It's a great way to use triangles that would otherwise be discarded.

. . . .

equinox

Simple style, big impact. Constructed without binding, this geometric table runner will add a modern touch to your decor. Channel quilting—parallel lines stitched close together—accentuates the modern look.

›› **BY MICHELLE BARTHOLOMEW**

›› **Finished table runner:** 18" × 43½"

materials

Yardage is based on 42"-wide fabric.

- ⅞ yard of white solid for flying-geese units, inner border, and sashing
- ¼ yard *each* of gray, chartreuse, and green solids for flying-geese units
- ⅛ yard *each* of blue and aqua solids for flying-geese units
- ¼ yard *each* of peach and pink solids for flying-geese units and sashing
- ⅓ yard of dark green solid for flying-geese units and outer border
- 1⅜ yards of fabric for backing
- 23" × 48" piece of white flannel for batting

cutting

All measurements include ¼"-wide seam allowances.

From the white solid, cut:
1 strip, 3" × 42"; crosscut into 6 squares, 3" × 3"
7 strips, 2½" × 42"; crosscut into:
    2 strips, 2½" × 20½"
    6 rectangles, 2½" × 4½"
    84 squares, 2½" × 2½"
1 strip, 1¾" × 42"; crosscut into 2 strips, 1¾" × 16½"
2 strips, 1¼" × 42"; crosscut into 4 strips, 1¼ " × 16½"

From *each* of the gray, chartreuse, and green solids, cut:
10 rectangles, 2½" × 4½" (30 total)
1 square, 3" × 3" (3 total)

From *each* of the blue and aqua solids, cut:
1 square, 3" × 3" (2 total)
2 rectangles, 2½" × 4½" (4 total)

From the peach solid, cut:
1 square, 3" × 3"
2 rectangles, 2½" × 4½"
2 strips, 1½" × 16½"

From the pink solid, cut:
2 rectangles, 2½" × 4½"
2 strips, 1½" × 16½"

From the dark green solid, cut:
4 strips, 1½" × 42"
2 rectangles, 2½" × 4½"

making the blocks

Press all seam allowances as shown by the arrows in the illustrations or as noted in the instructions.

1 Draw a diagonal line from corner to corner on the wrong side of each white 2½" square. Place a marked square on one end of a gray 2½" × 4½" rectangle, right sides together. Stitch on the line; trim away the excess fabric, leaving a ¼" seam allowance, and press.

2. Place a second marked white square on the opposite end of the unit made in step 1, right sides together. Stitch, trim, and press to complete a flying-geese unit that measures 2½" × 4½", including seam allowances.

Make 1 flying-geese unit, 2½" x 4½".

3. Repeat steps 1 and 2 to make a total of 40 flying-geese units (10 each of gray, chartreuse, and green, and two each of blue, aqua, peach, pink, and dark green).

4. Draw a diagonal line from corner to corner on the wrong side of each white 3" square. Place a marked white square on a gray 3" square, right sides together. Sew ¼" from both sides of the line. Cut on the drawn line to yield two half-square-triangle units. Trim the units to 2½" square. Repeat to make a total of 12 half-square-triangle units (two each of gray, chartreuse, green, blue, aqua, and peach).

Make 12 total units.

assembling the table-runner top

1. Lay out four each of gray, chartreuse, and green flying-geese units, two white 1¼" × 16½" strips, one peach 1½" × 16½" strip, one pink 1½" × 16½" strip, and one white 1¾" × 16½" strip in eight rows as shown. Join the flying-geese units in each row. Join the rows to make an end unit. Make two end units that measure 11¼" × 16½", including seam allowances.

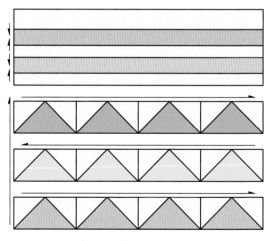

Make 2 end units, 11¼" x 16½".

2 Lay out the remaining flying-geese units, half-square-triangle units, white 2½" × 4½" rectangles, and white 2½" squares in 10 rows as shown. Join the pieces in each row. Press all seam allowances open. Join the rows. Add the white 2½" × 20½" strips to the long sides of the unit to make the center unit, which should measure 16½" × 20½", including seam allowances.

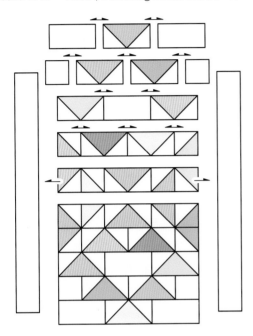

3 Join the center unit and end units. The table-runner top should now measure 16½" × 42".

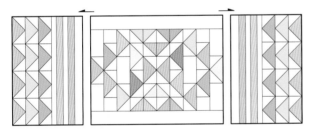

Runner assembly

easy spacing

Use the width of your machine's walking foot as a guide for spacing the quilting lines.

4 Join the dark green 1½"-wide strips end to end to make a long strip. From the long strip, cut two 42"-long border strips and two 18½"-long border strips. Sew the 42"-long strips to the long sides of the table-runner center. Add the 18½"-long strips to the remaining sides to complete the table-runner top, which should measure 18½" × 44".

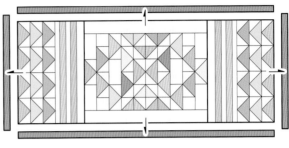

Adding borders,
18½" x 44"

finishing the table runner

For help with the following steps, find free, illustrated instructions at ShopMartingale.com/HowtoQuilt.

1 Place the table-runner top right side up on top of the flannel. Baste the layers together. Quilt the layers just enough to attach the table-runner top to the flannel. Trim the excess flannel even with the edges of the table-runner top.

2 Place the table runner on the backing fabric, right sides together. Pin all three layers together around the edges. Sew around all four sides with a ¼" seam allowance, leaving open a 6" section in the center of one long edge for turning.

3 Trim off the excess backing fabric and clip the corners to reduce bulk. Turn right side out through the opening, carefully poking out the corners with a chopstick. Turn under the raw edges of the opening and press flat. Using a ⅛" seam allowance, topstitch around the outer edge of the table runner, stitching the opening closed as you go.

4 Re-baste through all three layers. Complete the quilting as desired to attach the layers together. The runner shown is machine quilted with parallel lines spaced about ⅜" apart. See "Easy Spacing," left.

wonky triangles

Create a unique table runner using a nontraditional method of making triangles within a block. No two blocks look exactly the same! Simply layer two squares, make three cuts, and you're ready to go sew. » **BY MIRANDA ROSA**

» **Finished table runner:** 12½" × 60½"
   Finished blocks: 12" × 12" and 6" × 6"

materials

Yardage is based on 42"-wide fabric. Fat quarters measure 18" × 21".

- ¾ yard of blue solid for blocks
- ½ yard *each* of light gray solid and charcoal solid for blocks
- 1 fat quarter of dark gray solid for blocks
- ⅜ yard of medium gray solid for binding
- 1 yard of fabric for backing
- 17" × 65" piece of batting

cutting

All measurements include ¼"-wide seam allowances.

From the blue solid, cut:
2 squares, 14" × 14"
4 squares, 8½" × 8½"

From *each* of the light gray and charcoal solids, cut:
1 square, 14" × 14" (2 total)
2 squares, 8½" × 8½" (4 total)

From the dark gray solid, cut:
2 squares, 8½" × 8½"

From the medium gray solid, cut:
4 strips, 2½" × 42"

making the blocks

Press all seam allowances as shown by the arrows in the illustrations.

1 Place a blue 14" square on top of a light gray 14" square on a cutting mat. Make three cuts as shown to make a triangle. Make sure the second and third cuts are at least 1" from the fabric edge. (Finishing the cut too close to the edge of the fabric may result in a triangle corner being sewn into the seam allowance and disappearing.)

Cut 1.   Cut 2.   Cut 3.

2 Swap the blue and gray triangles. Sewing in the reverse order from which you cut, sew the pieces back together with a light gray triangle inside a blue square for one Large block. Sew a second Large block with a blue triangle inside a light gray square. Trim the blocks to 12½" square.

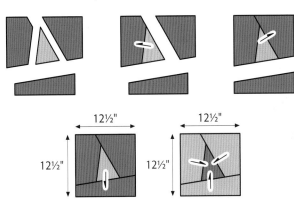

Make 2 Large blocks.

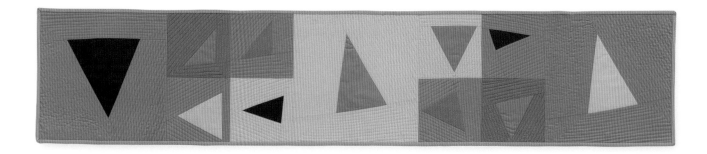

3 Repeat steps 1 and 2 with a pair of blue and charcoal 14" squares. Trim the blocks to 12½" square. Keep the blue block with the charcoal triangle, and set aside the other block (see "Extras!" below right for ideas).

4 Using blue and dark gray 8½" squares, repeat steps 1 and 2 to cut, swap fabrics, and assemble four blue and dark gray Small blocks. Trim the blocks to 6½" square.

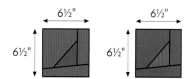

Make 2 of each Small block.

5 Repeat step 4 to make two Small blocks *each* of blue and charcoal, light gray and charcoal, and blue and light gray. Trim the blocks to 6½" square.

assembling the table-runner top

1 Referring to the runner assembly diagram, lay out the three Large blocks and eight Small blocks of your choosing. Join the Small blocks into rows; press.

2 Join the Large blocks and the Small-block rows to make the table-runner top, which should measure 12½" × 60½".

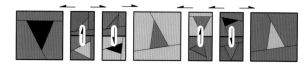

Runner assembly

finishing the table runner

For help with the following steps, find free, illustrated instructions at ShopMartingale.com/HowtoQuilt.

1 Prepare the backing so it's about 4" larger in both directions than the table-runner top. Layer the backing, batting, and table-runner top. Baste the layers together.

2 Hand or machine quilt; the runner shown is machine quilted with closely spaced lines of echo quilting around the triangles.

3 Use the medium gray 2½"-wide strips to make the binding, and then attach it to the runner.

extras!

Because these blocks are made in pairs, you'll have extra blocks. Use the extras to make another runner, to extend the length of this runner, or to make pillows, pot holders or table toppers!

olive tree

Inspired by the olive, a staple in many homes, this runner features curvy leaves and olives in a modern setting. The dimensional curves are entirely made from folded inserts—no need to cut or sew curves! » **BY ANNETTE ORNELAS**

Finished table runner: 21½" × 32½"
Finished blocks: 6" × 10" and 10" × 10"

materials

Yardage is based on 42"-wide fabric.

- ¼ yard of dark green batik for blocks
- ½ yard of light green batik for blocks and binding
- 1 yard of cream batik for background
- 1 rectangle, at least 6" × 8", of purple batik for blocks
- ⅞ yard of fabric for backing
- 26" × 37" piece of batting
- Glue stick or glue pen

cutting

All measurements include ¼"-wide seam allowances.

From the dark green batik, cut:
2 strips, 2½" × 42"; crosscut into:
    2 rectangles, 2½" × 8½"
    4 rectangles, 2½" × 6½"
    3 rectangles, 2½" × 4½"
    6 squares, 2½" × 2½"

From the light green batik, cut:
1 strip, 2½" × 42"; crosscut into:
    2 rectangles, 2½" × 6½"
    1 rectangle, 2½" × 4½"
    2 squares, 2½" × 2½"

From the remainder of the light green batik, cut:
Enough 2"-wide bias strips to total 120" in length when joined for binding

From the cream batik, cut:
2 strips, 6½" × 42"; crosscut into:
    2 rectangles, 6½" × 8½"
    4 rectangles, 4½" × 6½"
    4 rectangles, 2½" × 6½"
1 strip, 5½" × 42"; crosscut into 2 rectangles, 5½" × 10½"
1 strip, 4½" × 42"; crosscut into:
    4 squares, 4½" × 4½"
    4 rectangles, 2½" × 4½"
2 strips, 2½" × 42"; crosscut into:
    28 squares, 2½" × 2½"
    6 rectangles, 1½" × 2½"
2 strips, 1½" × 42"; crosscut into:
    1 strip, 1½" × 32½"
    2 strips, 1½" × 10½"
    16 squares, 1½" × 1½"

From the purple batik, cut:
2 rectangles, 2½" × 3½"
2 squares, 2½" × 2½"

preparing the triangles

Each dimensional curve is made from a folded square of fabric, which is placed on a base piece and sewn into the seams. Fold the following squares into triangles, and then press them with a warm iron to keep the folded shape.

- Fold 6 dark green and 2 light green 2½" squares diagonally to make 8 green 2½" folded triangles.
- Fold 24 cream 2½" squares diagonally to make 24 cream 2½" folded triangles.
- Fold 16 cream 1½" squares diagonally to make 16 cream 1½" folded triangles.

Make 8.

Make 24.

Make 16.

layering folded triangles

Place the folded triangles on the base pieces as instructed. Match the 90° corner of the folded triangles to the 90° corner of the base pieces, and adhere the triangles with a dab of glue at the corners to temporarily keep them in place.

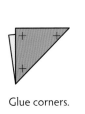

Glue corners.

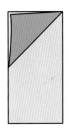

Match corners.

making the olive blocks

Press all seam allowances as shown by the arrows in the illustrations.

1 Place a cream 1½" folded triangle on each corner of a purple 2½" square as shown. Adhere the folded triangles with a dab of glue at the corners. The folded points will overlap along the sides of the square. Make two.

Make 2.

2 Sew cream 1½" × 2½" rectangles to opposite edges of a unit from step 1 to make a Small Olive block. Make two Small Olive blocks that measure 4½" × 2½", including seam allowances.

Small Olive block.
Make 2 blocks, 4½" x 2½".

3 Position and glue baste a cream 1½" folded triangle on each corner of a purple 2½" × 3½" rectangle as shown. Make two.

Make 2.

4 Sew a cream 2½" square and a cream 1½" × 2½" rectangle to the short edges of a unit from step 3 to make a large olive unit. Sew a cream 6½" × 8½" rectangle to the unit to make a Large Olive block. Make two Large Olive blocks that measure 10½" × 6½", including seam allowances.

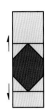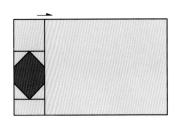

Large Olive block.
Make 2 blocks, 10½" x 6½".

making the leaf blocks

1 Position and glue baste a cream 2½" folded triangle on the upper-left and lower-right corners of a dark green 2½" × 4½" rectangle. Position and glue baste a dark green 2½" folded triangle on the upper-left corner of a cream 2½" × 4½" rectangle as shown. Sew the rectangles together and add a cream 4½" × 6½" rectangle to make an A unit that measures 4½" × 10½", including seam allowances. Repeat to make a light green A unit.

 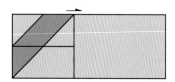

Unit A.
Make 1 unit, 4½" x 10½".

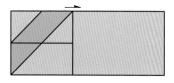

Unit A.
Make 1 unit, 4½" x 10½".

2 Position and glue baste a cream 2½" folded triangle on the upper-left and lower-right corners of a dark green 2½" × 6½" rectangle. Position and glue baste a dark green 2½" folded triangle on the upper-left corner of a cream 2½" × 6½" rectangle as shown. Sew the rectangles together and add a cream 4½" square to make a B unit. Make two dark green B units that measure 4½" × 10½", including seam allowances.

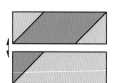

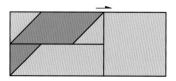

Unit B.
Make 2 units, 4½" x 10½".

3 Position and glue baste a cream 2½" folded triangle on the upper-left and lower-right corners of a dark green 2½" × 8½" rectangle. Add a cream 2½" square to the right side to make a C unit. Make two dark green C units that measure 2½" × 10½", including seam allowances.

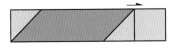

Unit C.
Make 2 units, 2½" x 10½".

4 Sew A, B, and C units together as shown to make a Leaf block. Press the seam allowances away from the layered pieces or press them open when necessary to avoid bulk. Make two Leaf blocks that measure 10½" square, including seam allowances.

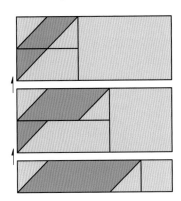

Leaf block.
Make 1 block, 10½" x 10½".

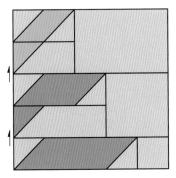

Leaf block.
Make 1 block, 10½" x 10½".

making the leaf-and-olive blocks

1 Position and glue baste a cream 2½" folded triangle on the lower-left and top-right corners of a dark green 2½" × 6½" rectangle as shown. Add a Small Olive block to the right side to make a D unit that measures 2½" × 10½", including seam allowances. Repeat to make a light green D unit.

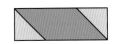
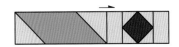

Unit D.
Make 1 unit, 2½" x 10½".

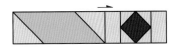

Unit D.
Make 1 unit, 2½" x 10½".

2 Position and glue baste a dark green 2½" folded triangle on the lower-left corner of a cream 2½" × 6½" rectangle. Position and glue baste a cream 2½" folded triangle on the lower-left and top-right corners of a dark green 2½" × 6½" rectangle. Sew the rectangles together and add a cream 4½" square to make an E unit that measures 4½" × 10½", including seam allowances. Repeat to make a light green E unit.

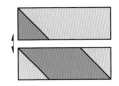
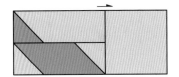

Unit E.
Make 1 unit, 4½" x 10½".

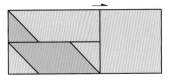

Unit E.
Make 1 unit, 4½" x 10½".

3 Position and glue baste a dark green 2½" folded triangle on the lower-left corner of a cream 2½" × 4½" rectangle. Position and glue baste a cream 2½" folded triangle on the lower-left and top-right corners of a dark green 2½" × 4½" rectangle. Sew the

rectangles together and add a cream 4½" × 6½" rectangle to make an F unit that measures 4½" × 10½", including seam allowances. Make two dark green F units.

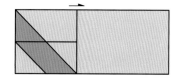

Unit F.
Make 2 units, 4½" x 10½".

4 Sew units D, E, and F together as shown to make a Leaf-and-Olive block. Press the seam allowances away from layered pieces or press them open when necessary to avoid bulk. Repeat to make two Leaf-and-Olive blocks that measure 10½" square, including seam allowances.

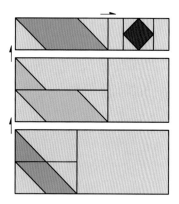

Leaf-and-Olive block.
Make 1 block, 10½" x 10½".

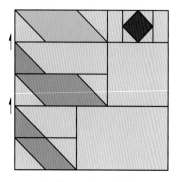

Leaf-and-Olive block.
Make 1 block, 10½" x 10½".

assembling the table-runner top

1 Lay out the Large Olive blocks, Leaf blocks, Leaf-and-Olive blocks, cream 1½" × 10½" strips, and cream 5½" × 10½" rectangles in three vertical rows as shown below. Join the pieces in each row.

2 Sew the cream 1½" × 32½" strip between the rows to make the table-runner top. The top should measure 21½" × 32½".

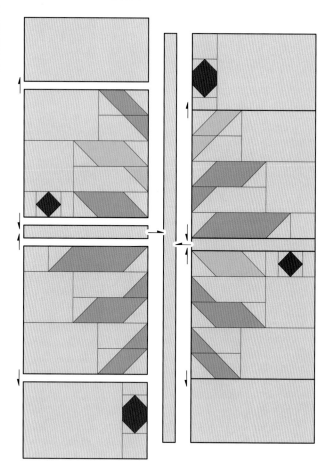

Runner assembly

topstitching the curves

Curves are made by folding back and manipulating the folded triangles. The folded edges are bias edges, and you can easily peel them back, smooth them into a curved shape, and then topstitch to make the curves permanent. Use a sewing machine to topstitch the curves or use hand appliqué. Finishing the curves by hand makes this a great take-along project.

Topstitching by machine. Insert the sewing-machine needle in the starting point of a fold to hold the quilt top in place. Lock the stitches by stitching in place, and then carefully fold back the bias edge. Smooth out the curve and hold it down with a stiletto while carefully stitching close to its outer edge with a straight stitch. Lock the stitches again at the end of the curve, and then move to the next folded triangle.

Topstitching by hand. Use an appliqué stitch or invisible stitch to secure each folded edge. Always match your thread to the folded piece for best results.

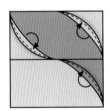

thread, needles, and sewing-machine feet

For topstitching by machine, use a fine-weight thread that matches each fabric to be topstitched. Cotton embroidery-weight thread works well. Sharp sewing-machine needles made for woven fabrics work best to stitch through all the layers. Use an open-toe foot or a clear machine foot that allows you to see the needle as it enters the fabric.

. . . .

finishing the table runner

For help with the following steps, find free, illustrated instructions at ShopMartingale.com/HowtoQuilt.

1 Prepare the backing so it's about 4" larger in both directions than the table-runner top. Layer the backing, batting, and table-runner top. Baste the layers together.

2 Hand or machine quilt; the runner shown is machine quilted with spirals of assorted sizes in the background. (See "Topstitching the Curves During Quilting" below). After the table runner is quilted, trace a small saucer or lid on each corner and trim on the line to round the corners.

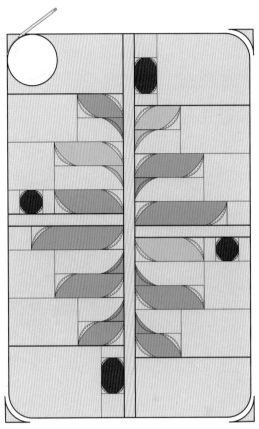

Trimming corners.

topstitching the curves during quilting

Small projects such as table runners can be topstitched during the quilting process. First, pin baste or spray baste the table runner with batting and backing. Then peel back all the loose pieces and topstitch by machine as shown above. Make this table runner extra quick to finish by stitching in the ditch along the seams to quilt from one curve to the next.

. . . .

3 Use the light green 2"-wide bias strips to make the binding, and then attach it to the runner.

about the contributors

MICHELLE BARTHOLOMEW

Michelle is a self-taught quilter who has always had a desire to create. A photographer and technical writer, Michelle provides interviews and inspiration for quilters each month via her modern-quilting newsletter, *Half-Square Headlines*. Visit her at MichelleBartholomew.com.

DEANE BEESLEY

Deane grew up surrounded by creative and inspiring people, and she learned a variety of crafts as a child. When she took a quilting class in her early twenties, Deane knew she had found her calling. She eventually became the owner of her own quilting store, and her passion for creativity led to a career in fabric design. Visit SweetBeeDesigns.com.

JANE DAVIDSON

Jane's love affair with quilting started when she was a teenager. She has no fear of color and loves to add vibrant prints and textures to her quilts. Together Jane and Pat Sloan created The Splendid Sampler Sew-Along. Jane enjoys traveling to teach and meeting enthusiastic quilters from all over the world. Visit QuiltJane.com.

TONY JACOBSON

A nationally known quilt designer, Tony learned to quilt from his grandmother at age 10. In addition to running a quilt shop and working for the Quilts of Valor Foundation, Tony also enjoys teaching. He constantly searches for techniques that will make the quilting process faster, easier, and more accurate. Visit PieceWorksQuiltShop.com.

KIM LAPACEK

Kim is a mother, wife, artist, and retired civil engineer. In the fall she can be found working in her apple orchard's shop. A huge fan of online quilt-alongs, she dreamed up Project Quilting in 2010. She shares her enthusiasm about creativity through teaching, lecturing, and blogging. Visit KimLapacek.com.

ANNETTE ORNELAS

Annette is a German-born quilt artist, teacher, and designer living in North Carolina. She enjoys gardening, taking motorcycle trips with her husband, and providing workshops and lectures throughout the US. Her techniques enable quilters of all skill levels to make complex-looking designs using her easy methods of straight-line piecing with curved results. Visit SouthWindQuilts.com.

SUE PFAU

Sue first started quilting as a flight attendant, bringing hand appliqué on flights. In 2006 she began making and selling quilts but had a hard time finding patterns that were quick and easy yet also beautiful and interesting. So she began designing her own. This led to her design company, which is called Sweet Jane's Quilting and Design after her daughter, Jane. Visit Sue online at SweetJanesQuilting.blogspot.com or her shop at SweetJane.etsy.com.

MIRANDA ROSA

Miranda first learned to sew at the age of nine. When her parents opened a quilt shop during her teen years, she was hooked. Over the years she has made many quilts and accessories, and she shares her enthusiasm for modern and contemporary designs on her blog. Visit Miranda at MyBitofWonder.com.

JUDE SPERO

Raised by her grandmother, who was an avid sewist, Jude grew up surrounded by piles of fabric. As a child she sewed doll clothes and blankets. In the early 1970s she started quilting and then became a long-arm quilter and quilt shop owner. Designing quilts is what she enjoys most. Visit Jude at LittleLouiseDesigns.com.

JULIE TAYLOR

Needlecrafts were an intrinsic part of family life as Julie grew up, and her love for them has grown stronger as she's grown older. Enjoying both modern and traditional quilting, Julie likes to add a contemporary twist to well-loved designs. Creating something with fabric is her favorite way of relaxing, and new ideas pop into her head while she's quietly sewing. "If only I could make them as fast as I dream them up!" she says. Visit Julie at Instagram (@mackandmabel) to see what she's currently making, and at MackandMabelPatterns.com.